C000129761

Maxims of Christian
Perfection

Antonio Rosmini

Edited by

A. Belsito

CONTENT

Cover and drawings by P.M. Rodrigues

ISBN 978-1-899093-24-3

Rosmini Centre
433 Fosse Way
Ratcliffe-on-the-Wreake LE7 4SJ
Email: aabelsito@hotmail.com
www.rosminicentre.co.uk

INTRODUCTION

"There were six stone water jars standing there"
(John 2, 6)

Blessed Rosmini is not famed for writing short books. His over 100 volumes, dealing with all branches of philosophy – from epistemology to ethics, from metaphysics to anthropology, from psychology to the philosophy of Right – and with theology and spirituality, are normally substantial books. Even his letters have been collected in 13 large volumes.

It is a pleasant surprise, therefore, to know that his acknowledged master-piece on spirituality is a short booklet of just about 40 pages, written for the benefit of religious and lay people alike, "for people in all conditions of life", as Blessed Rosmini puts it. In effect, the booklet has been read and appreciated by many famous people as well, Newman, Manzoni, St. Magdalene of Canossa, Pope John XXIII, Von Balthasar, and many others, who have left moving testimonies about the power, the depth, the simplicity, and beauty of its content.

The spirituality of Blessed Rosmini has its profound roots in the Scriptures, in the Gospels in particular. Of his substantial book, "The Constitutions of the Institute of Charity", which he considered an expansion of the Maxims of Christian Perfection, he wrote: *"With the rest of the faithful we have the Gospel of Christ as our great common book. We must use it day and night. Our Constitutions, taken from the Gospel, must lead us back to it"* (C464E).

It comes natural to think of the six Maxims as the *"six jars full of excellent wine"*, like the six jars at Cana of Galilee after the first miracle of JESUS. The rich juices from the Gospel are to be found in the six precious Maxims, each giving that which is "essential", fundamental in our spiritual life, that without which our spiritual life is either non-existent or is severely warped.

"Only one thing is necessary", said the Lord to Martha. He Himself provided the explanation when He said, *"What will it profit a man, if he gains the whole world and forfeits his soul? Or what shall a man give in return for his soul?"* The Scriptures leave us in no doubt that "the salvation and perfection" of our soul should be our primary occupation in life, the end for the sake of which we do all other things.

"We must be convinced that there is only one thing which is necessary – porro unum est necessarium – and this one thing is the salvation of our soul", thus wrote Blessed Rosmini; and again, *"Goodness is the eternal salvation of the soul, and its moral perfection"*; and again, *"The salvation of the soul is that treasure we must own by selling all other possessions,*

as the Gospel says; *it is more valuable than anything else, and possessing it one possesses all things*" (Letters, passim).

Blessed Rosmini founded the Institute of Charity and the sisters of Providence with only one purpose in mind: the salvation and the perfection of the members. This is what he wrote in the Constitutions:

"The end of this Society is to care lovingly for the sanctification of the members who compose it and, by means of their sanctification, to expend whatever longings and strength it has in all works of charity, and especially for the eternal salvation of every one of its neighbours."

"The Institute consists of faithful Christians who, in their ardent desire of living as disciples of JESUS Christ, our Lord and Master, apply themselves vigorously, with mutual help and encouragement, to their own perfection."

A few days before his death, Blessed Rosmini left to his friend Tommaseo this simple advice: *"Our task in life is to pursue the great business of saving our soul."*

The salvation and perfection of the soul is, therefore, that "simple principle and seed" which will give unity to all our endeavors in life. Holiness is, for us, the salvation and perfection of the soul, and the command to pursue holiness comes directly from JESUS Himself: *"Be perfect, as your heavenly Father is perfect"*, a command which is addressed to all.

Holiness, in Scriptures, is often called *"justice"*; Joseph, for example, was described by Matthew as a *"just man"*. And JESUS invites us to *"seek first the Kingdom of God and its justice"*, and again, *"Blessed are those who hunger and thirst for justice, for they shall be satisfied"*.

There is a great advantage in calling holiness "justice", since it may seem to many that "holiness" is something reserved to a few great souls, whereas the word "justice" demands at once that everyone be "just". It is easy to understand that justice is something to which everyone is called, it is not an optional extra, something reserved to few selected souls; the duty to be just – holy – is a categorical imperative for everyone.

But what is justice? Blessed Rosmini developed the theme by considering three aspects that together make up justice:

1- Justice is "abstaining from sin", is a life-long struggle to remove from our lives, with God's grace, whatever resists God's holiness, a constant process of purification. Under this aspect justice is purity, innocence of life, is putting truth at the centre of our heart and mind. Justice is to have a heart which is free from sin: pride, mendacity, passions, selfishness.

2- Justice is to know and to acknowledge the order of being, giving what is due to everyone and everything. This is God's justice in the first place, since He is absolute real Being, the creator of all that is. God,

Absolute Being, is Love and God loves all that He has created, according to the order of creation.

Justice in this sense compels us to give God the adoration, obedience and love which are due to Him as our Creator, our sovereign Lord and Master, our infinite benefactor and heavenly Father; and to give to ourselves and to all creatures whatever God has ordained to be due to us and to them. All virtues are based on justice, that is, on acknowledging and loving the truth of all beings as they are in themselves. This is what Blessed Rosmini says about this meaning of justice:

"Justice consists in giving to all their own, in recognising and loving everything for what it is, neither more nor less. The innate light of reason, and more importantly the light of faith, shows that God is the Supreme Being, infinitely greater than all the beings which are his creatures. He is, therefore, worthy to be infinitely esteemed and loved above them all" (Rosmini, Manuale dell'Esercitatore).

3- Justice is Calvary, the hill of blood. Calvary is the "sublime altar" empurpled by the precious Blood flowing from the veins of Christ satisfying the Father's eternal justice and bringing salvation to all. Calvary is a place of shame, but it was there that the sin of the world was taken away by the sacrifice of love of the Lamb of God. Calvary, therefore, is the hill of "justice": the hill where all sins were taken away by the Blood of the Son of God, the hill that manifested the infinite love of God for us – *"God did not spare His only Son, but gave Him up to benefit us all"*

(Rom. 8, 32) -, the hill from which all the means of salvation have come to us. The Church came forth from the open side of Christ, the new Adam, and with the Church, the two great sacraments, baptism and the Eucharist, represented by the water and the blood. We can truly say, *"Blessed is the wood by which justice came"* (Wisdom 14, 7).

This lofty view of justice explains the reason for the first Maxim: *"To desire only and without limit to please God, that is, to be just"*. This Maxim calls for the constant purification of our soul, for the daily practice of all virtues, and for intimate union and love of God. In a word, it calls for justice, for holiness; and since holiness comes from God, the simple task of the Christian is to desire justice at all times, and to ask for it in humble and persistent prayer.

It is easy to understand the connection between justice and the Will of God, manifested in what we call Divine Providence. To act justly is to act in perfect conformity with the Will of God, our Maker; hence holiness is nothing but the constant striving of the soul to know and to do the Will of God in all things.

And first of all it is the Will of God that we love the Church, since she is the beloved Bride of God's Son, and in the Church that which is an essential part, the Holy See. We can never go wrong when we put love for the Church and for the Holy Father as priorities in our life, since we are certain that this is the Will of God.

The constant search for the Will of God should extend to all moments of our life, to the big occasions – should I become a religious, or a priest, or a married person, a doctor or a nurse, etc. – and to the daily occurrences such as – which work of charity should I do? Which person should I help? How to be more useful to my neighbour? How does the Lord wish me to organise my day, my activities, or my life of prayer? Etc.

We have three certainties about the Will of God: firstly, it is certain that God wants me to engage with all my strength in pursuing the "salvation and perfection" of my soul; secondly, it is equally certain that I should love the Church, His Bride, with commitment and enthusiasm, ready to toil and to shed my blood for her. Thirdly, it is the Will of the Saviour that I should love and respect the Successor of St. Peter, the Pope, the "rock" on which Christ's Church has been built.

But, how do we come to know the Will of God concerning both the big choices we are called to make, and the daily ones?

The answer is firstly to abandon ourselves to Divine Providence with trust, love, and peace of heart. The Lord speaks to us at all times and in many ways, and we need to listen carefully to His voice. He does not speak in a timid, confused manner, it is more like the "roar of the lion", as Amos says. For Blessed Rosmini, the voice of God was the voice of Pius VIII telling him,

"It is the will of God that you write books, this is your vocation. The Church has a great need of writers, I mean, solid writers so extremely few in numbers. In order to influence people usefully there is no other means today but to take them by means of reason, and by this means to lead them to religion. Be assured that you will benefit your neighbour far more successfully by writing than by any other work of pastoral ministry" (Rosmini, Introduction to Philosophy).

Blessed Rosmini came to know the Will of God about the founding of the Institute from the clear words of St. Magdalene of Canossa, of a French priest, Fr. Loewenbruck, and finally from Pope Pius VIII. He never had any doubt about his double mission in life: God had expressed His Will clearly and powerfully not through direct revelation, but through providential people and events.

But whilst we make our ears attentive, like the young Samuel, to listen to the word of God, we ought to remain at the same time totally immersed in our primary task in life, the salvation and perfection of our soul. The contemplative life should be, normally, the first state of every Christian, an "active" contemplative life, totally dedicated to pursuing the salvation and perfection of the soul.

It will be Divine Providence to indicate to us God's Will clearly: we shall maintain a perfect indifference as to whatever the Will of God will ask of us, without any interference on our part. Only then we will be able to repeat with JESUS, *"I have come not to do my will, but the Will of my Father in heaven"*, or *"My food is to do the Will of my Father"*, or *"I have come, Lord, to do your Will"*.

By acknowledging our own nothingness, we shall place all our trust in God; and by knowing how small we are in the spiritual life, we shall not presume to do great works for the Church or for our brothers and sisters. We shall concentrate on purifying our soul until the Lord will indicate His Will concerning our spiritual mission. Once the Lord reveals His Will to us, then we shall put our trust in Him, and He will give us the means to fulfil His Will: *"You shall perform even greater works"*, said the Lord.

Blessed Rosmini, in the sixth Maxim, insists on the "spirit of intelligence", as the favourite means to ascertain the Will of God in all our occupations. This should not be a surprise for those who have been initiated into his philosophy, since they would know that intelligence is, for Blessed Rosmini, the link between man and God, is the "divine in nature", in the sense that the innate idea of being, which is what makes us intelligent, comes directly from God, is the "light that enlightens every man who comes into this world".

The proper use of reason is the golden means given to natural man of discovering God and His Will, by reading carefully the circumstances, the events, the persons we encounter in our daily life. Supernatural grace strengthens our spirit of intelligence, enabling it to perceive the Will of God more readily and more clearly. Blessed Rosmini wrote in the Constitutions, *"Our life will be perfect when we do all things according to the light of reason. Our actions must depend upon the indications and necessity offered by reason itself, not upon caprice. We must remain at rest, then, until moved by reason"* (C484).

The Maxims came into being as the result of a profound religious experience, soon after his ordination to the priesthood at the age of 24, which led Blessed Rosmini from a previous hectic life of initiatives in defense of the Catholic Church, to a life of withdrawal from the world, of intense prayer, and of contemplation, in his paternal home at Rovereto, guided by two principles which became his rule of conduct:

"I, Antonio Rosmini, unworthy priest, have resolved to follow a rule of conduct consisting in the following two principles:

a. *To attend seriously to the task of correcting my enormous vices and of purifying my soul of the iniquity that has weighed upon it from my birth, without going in search of other occupations or undertakings for the benefit of my neighbour, finding myself quite impotent to do anything of myself to his advantage;*

b. *Never to turn down works of charity towards my neighbour, when divine Providence should offer and present them to me, for God has the power to use anyone and even myself for his works: in such cases I would maintain a perfect indifference in regard to all works of charity, doing the one proposed to me with the same enthusiasm as I would any other, at least as far as my free will is concerned".*

In its stark simplicity, this statement hides the whole wealth of Rosminian spirituality, the principle of passivity, the principle of indifference, trust in Divine Providence, the constant pursuit of the Will of God, humility, truth, etc. The six Maxims are an extended version of the above rule of conduct, as it is easy to see from the following table:

RULE OF CONDUCT (Principle of Passivity)	MAXIMS OF CHRISTIAN PERFECTION
1- To attend seriously to the task of correcting my enormous vices and of purifying my soul of the iniquity that has weighed upon it from my birth, without going in search of other occupations or undertakings for the benefit of my neighbour, finding myself quite impotent to do anything of myself to his advantage	1- To desire only and without limit to please God, that is to be just 2- To direct all our thoughts and actions to the increase, and to the glory, of the Church of JESUS Christ 3- To remain perfectly at peace as to all that is ordained by God in regard to the Church of Jesus Christ, working for the Church in obedience to the divine Will.
(Principle of indifference)	
2- Never to turn down works of charity towards my neighbour, when Divine Providence should offer and present them to me, for God has the power to use anyone and even myself for his works: in such cases I would maintain a perfect indifference in regard to all works of charity, doing the one proposed to me with the same enthusiasm as I would any other, at least as far as my free will is concerned.	4- To abandon ourselves completely to Divine Providence 5- To acknowledge profoundly our own nothingness 6- To regulate all the occupations of our life with a spirit of intelligence

The booklet, Maxims of Christian Perfection, was published for the first time in 1830, in Rome, capital of Christianity. Blessed Rosmini published there at the same time his great work, Essay on the Origin of Ideas, which is the foundational work of his philosophy. There was a precise reason for the place and the timing: he had wished to begin his vast production on philosophy, theology, and spirituality in obedience and submission to the Successor of St. Peter, the Holy Father, and to indicate that all his work would be at the service of the Church.

Blessed Rosmini considered the Maxims the essential core of the ascetical principles of his Institute of Charity, the seeds of the Constitutions: *"The Maxims contain the whole Institute of Charity in germ"* (Letters, III, 483). But he was also aware of the difficulty of grasping fully the richness of its content: *"The booklet must be read over and again with the greatest attention, since one cannot appreciate it without, as it were, chewing and masticating its content"* (Letters, I, 424); *"It is necessary that you assimilate and savour the content of the Maxims; it is not sufficient to read the booklet once, I have seen excellent results only after repeated reading"* (Letters, I, 426); *"The booklet of the Maxims is nothing but the essence of the Gospel, and it could become a more useful spiritual tool than any other"* (Letters, VII, 161).

We conclude this Introduction with the words of Tommaseo, a great Italian writer and friend of Blessed Rosmini, in a letter he wrote to him:

"Your book, the Maxims, contains most beautiful things; and it is of great importance that in a world full of decadence there should be someone who speaks of Christian perfection, with truly evangelical simplicity".

Maxims
of Christian
Perfection
Common to all
Christians

"There were six stone water jars standing there"
(St. John 2, 6)

"O Lord, You are my portion: I have
said that I will keep Your Law"
(Psalm 118, 57)

How to read profitably this booklet

JESUS said, "One only is your Master". Before starting to read, let the disciples sit at the feet of their Master with eagerness, and as they read let them hear the voice of JESUS speaking to them.

Let them begin with the sign of the Cross and the Lord's Prayer, the Our Father.

As they read, let them pay attention to the following:

1 To understand fully the meaning of what is written

2 To reflect in depth, and to savour in their hearts what they had been reading

Let them propose, at the end, to keep what they have learned, giving thanks to God, and reciting the Hail Mary.

INTRODUCTION

The Perfect Life in general

1- All Christians, that is, all disciples of JESUS Christ, are called to perfection, no matter what their state or condition may be; for all are called to the Gospel, which is a law of perfection; and to all alike was said by our Divine Master, "You must be perfect, as your heavenly Father is perfect" (Mt. 5, 48).

2- The perfection of the Gospel consists in the fulfilment of the two commandments of love, of God and of neighbour. This is the source of the desire and of the effort Christians make to abide in God with all their affections and actions, as much as is possible in this world, and in obedience to the commands, "You shall love the Lord your God with all your heart, and with all your soul, and with all your mind" and "You shall love your neighbour as yourself" (Mt. 22, 37.39).

3- To achieve this *perfection of love*, which should be the constant aim of the disciples of JESUS Christ, there are three very useful means, that is, the profession of genuine poverty, chastity, and obedience. These are not commands for every Christian; they are only counsels which the Gospel gives, and which have the power to remove from the mind, heart, and life of Christians whatever obstacle there may be to their committing themselves completely to the love of God and of neighbour.

4- The profession of the three evangelical counsels constitutes what is called *religious perfection*, not common to all Christians, but proper only to those generous disciples of JESUS who give up in actual fact wealth, pleasures, and their own will, to be freer to give God and neighbour all their love.

5- The Religious, that is, the Christians who profess the three evangelical counsels of actual poverty, chastity, and obedience, must use these three means to increase the perfection of love to which their brethren, all other Christians, are equally called.

6- Christians who, though not professing the evangelical counsels, desire nonetheless that perfection of divine love to which they were consecrated and which they vowed to God in holy Baptism, must be careful, as the angelic Doctor says (Summa Th. II, II, 186, 2), not to despise what relates to the practice of the evangelical counsels, and must, moreover, acknowledge their excellence and esteem them, and wish to have that generosity of soul, and that spiritual understanding of the truth which draws people to practise means that are so well adapted to free their hearts from all the cares and obstacles that hinder them from directing their whole mind and life to God in charity.

Christians who live the secular life will sometime be tempted not to value adequately these Divine counsels, through a hidden prompting of self love, which refuses to accept in oneself a lesser generosity than in others. But it is only through humility, which will make them think little of themselves, as belonging in the Kingdom of God to a state much less noble than the Religious state, that they will become truly pleasing to God, and will make up for what is wanting in them of generosity and spiritual knowledge.

7- Perfect charity, in which consists the perfection of all Christians, brings the whole person into union with the Creator. It may be defined as a total consecration or sacrifice that some Christians make to God, in imitation of that Sacrifice which was made by the only-begotten Son, our Redeemer JESUS Christ. By this consecration they intend to have no other ultimate end in all their actions than the service of God; and to have no object, and to seek for no good or happiness on earth, except that of pleasing God and of serving Him.

8- Hence it follows that true Christians, who aspire to the perfection to which they are called, should resolve to do always, in all the actions of their life, what they believe to be most pleasing to God, tending most to His glory, and most in conformity with His will.

9. To discover, in the conduct of their life, what is in conformity with the Divine will, Christians ought always to have their eyes fixed, and their meditation directed, upon the Spirit of their Divine Master and upon His heavenly instruction.

10. This instruction comes under these two headings, to which the whole teaching of the Gospel may be reduced:

1. The END of our actions, which Christians ought ever to have in view, that they may follow it with the simplicity of the dove; and for this purpose we should have the most clear and distinct idea of it.

2. The MEANS by which, with the prudence of the serpent, we may attain that end.

As to the END, Christians should put before themselves, and continually meditate upon, three fundamental Maxims; and they ought also to put before themselves, and to meditate upon, three Maxims relative to the MEANS; in all, six Maxims, which are the following:

I   To desire only and without limit to please God, that is, to be just.

II   To direct all our thoughts and actions to the increase, and to the glory, of the Church of JESUS Christ.

III   To remain perfectly at peace as to all that is ordained by God in regard to the Church of JESUS Christ, working for the Church in obedience to the divine Will.

IV   To abandon ourselves completely to Divine Providence.

V   To acknowledge profoundly our own nothingness.

VI   To regulate all the occupations of our life with a spirit of intelligence.

❉ ❉

These six Maxims will form the content of the six following Instructions.

"There were six stone water jars standing there"
(St. John 2, 6)

First Maxim

"To desire only and without limit to please God, that is, to be just"

FIRST MAXIM

"To desire only and without limit to please God, that is, to be just"

1. Christians who love God in the way laid down by the Gospel, *with all their heart, and with all their mind, and with all their soul,* since they are unable to give anything good to God (for God has all that is good), desire at least to be *just* towards God by acknowledging His infinite perfection, and by rendering to Him, in all their actions, the greatest possible obedience, homage, submission, and adoration; that is to say, they desire only and without limit the glory of God. And, as in the homage and glory that are given to God consists the sanctity of the person, the perfection preached by Christianity implies an endeavor to attain the highest possible sanctity.

2. Now, the greatest homage that we can give to God consists in that submission of our will by which we desire only the greatest possible conformity of our own will to the Divine will; so that whatever is most pleasing to God, we at once are ready to prefer to all things else, having no wish but to become as dear to God as we can be, looking upon this as our only happiness, and asking for it without ceasing.

3. As it is *justice* that renders us dear to God, Christians should pray unceasingly that they may become more just, more holy. In this they must never rest satisfied and content. They must go on praying more and more, feeling sure that the more they pray

for it, the more dear will they be to God, encouraging themselves with those words: *"Blessed are those who hunger and thirst for justice, for they shall be satisfied"* (Mt. 5, 6).

In those who profess the Christian religion all things should be reduced to this one point: to desire to be far more just than they are, and to pray for it without ceasing, without measure or limit, so that they may be made one with JESUS, even as JESUS is one with the Father. They must not rest satisfied, nor be afraid of asking too much. They must leave it to the infinite goodness of the Divine Father to satisfy them, out of His boundless treasures, with spiritual riches. God will know how to do this; and He will do it the more abundantly, the more earnestly we pray that we may be made more and more just, and be more and more perfectly united with Him.

Of this JESUS assures them: *"If you ask the Father anything in My name, He will give it to you"* (John 16, 23). To this JESUS urges them by His own example; for, whatever degree of justice we may wish to ask of our Heavenly Father, we know that Christ has already asked it for us in a prayer which could not pass unanswered; and upon this justice, obtained by His prayer, Christ has founded the Church of the saints, which will never perish.

4. Here is the prayer of JESUS, by which the disciples should be encouraged to beseech their Heavenly Father to make them more and more just: *"I pray not only for these, but for those also who through their words will believe in me. May they all be one. Father,*

may they be one in us, as you are in me and I am in you, so that the world may believe it was you who sent me. I have given them the glory you gave to me, that they may be one as we are one. With me in them and you in me, may they be so completely one that the world will realize that it was you who sent me and that I have loved them as much as you loved me" (St. John 17, 20-23).

5. The disciples therefore should continue fervently to desire justice, until it can be said that they are consumed in charity, and that *it is not they who now live, but Christ lives in them*, as the Apostle says (Gal. 2, 20).

6. This desire for justice, without limit or measure, must be a desire that is pure and most sincere. This the disciples may obtain by constantly renewing the desire, and at the same time withdrawing in spirit from all exterior things into a perfect interior solitude. With this inward recollection they ought perseveringly to ask for this same desire, according to the words, *"Stay awake, praying at all times"* (St. Luke 21, 36). They ought also to examine, and see if the desire is so truly sincere and free from everything else that in all things they care for nothing but this alone – to become more holy, more just, that is, in other words, more dear to God and more pleasing to Him.

7. Christians must not in the least feel lost, or become disheartened, if external things make an impression on them. With inward recollection, they must then without ceasing renew their sole desire of justice,

until they shall resolutely wish for nothing on earth but for the sake of justice, thus doing what is most pleasing to God.

8. Christians must understand, though it is not easy, how to this one desire of justice all other desires should be subordinate. For, if they freely wish for anything whatsoever, they ought to wish it only in so far as it is in conformity with justice, and may make them more just, and not for any other value that it may have.

9. And because perfect justice comes directly from God, and from God only, they ought to have no affection for anything on earth unless they know it to be a means chosen by God for their sanctification. They should be very careful not to imagine, as too often happens, that this is the case on account of some secret affection for something they like. They ought rather to feel assured that, in the hands of God, all things become equally well adapted to the Divine purpose; that the Lord is often pleased to manifest His power by choosing as His instruments things that of their nature seem to be the least suitable; and that we ought not to form a judgment as to the aptness of human things, until God has made known to us His sovereign will concerning them.

10. In desiring to be perfectly dear to God, Christians desire for themselves all that is truly good; for, to be dear to God, they must necessarily desire these things also. In this desire therefore are included all possible good desires; so that Christians who have this great desire, implicitly desire the salvation of all their

brethren; and they desire it in the way in which it is pleasing to God and in conformity with His will.

"It is holiness that makes us dear to God"
(Steps at the Sacra of S. Michele, Turin)

Second Maxim

"To direct all our thoughts and actions to the increase, and to the glory, of the Church of JESUS Christ"

SECOND MAXIM

"To direct all our thoughts and actions to the increase, and to the glory, of the Church of JESUS Christ"

1. The first desire that is generated in the heart of Christians by the supreme desire of justice, is for the increase, and for the glory, of the Church of JESUS Christ.

They who desire *justice*, desire all possible glory of God, and everything whatsoever that is dear to God. But Christians know by faith that all the delight of the Heavenly Father is in JESUS Christ His only-begotten Son; and that the delight of the only-begotten Son JESUS Christ is in the Faithful who form His kingdom.

2. Christians therefore can never err when they set for themselves the whole Holy Church as the object of their affections, thoughts, desires, and actions. As to this, they know with certainty that it is the will of God that the Church should be the great means by which His holy name is to be fully glorified.

3. Christians may doubt, as to any particular thing, whether God wishes it to be, in one way or another, a means of His glory. But as to the whole Church of JESUS Christ they can have no doubt, because it has certainly been established as the great instrument, the great means, by which God is to be glorified before all intelligent creatures.

4. Christians cannot have the same certainty in regard to a part only, which is not essential to the great body of the Holy Church. The object, therefore, of all their affections should be the whole immaculate Spouse of JESUS Christ; and not anything that might form a part of the Church, but that has not been marked out by God as truly and permanently belonging to it.

That is, they ought not to love without limit or condition any particular means that, considered in itself, might, if God so wished, be conducive to His glory; for they know not whether God, Whose ways are hidden from the thoughts and eyes of people may not reject such means. But in regard to the whole Church there can be no doubt; for it was chosen by God as instrument of His glory, without possibility of change during the whole course of never-ending eternity.

If, then, Christians who intend to follow their vocation, and to attain perfection, are determined to seek only in all things the glory of JESUS Christ, they ought to employ all their powers in the service of the Church; to her they ought, in every way that they can, to devote their thoughts; in her service they should wish to wear out their strength, and, after the example of JESUS Christ and of the martyrs, to shed their blood.

5. The holy Church of JESUS Christ is divided into that part which is in the state of pilgrimage on earth; that which is at its destination in heaven; and that which is near to it, in purgatory. Christians know that these three parts of the Church will last as long as this

world shall last, and that the Church triumphant will last for ever; for all three have been chosen as the instrument and the abode of the glory of God, in JESUS Christ, the Head and Ruler of the Church. Christians therefore, as members of this august society, ought, in union with JESUS Christ, to love these three parts of the Church with unbounded affection, desiring to toil and to shed their blood in their service.

6. Christians know, by the words of JESUS Christ, that the Church on the earth is founded upon a Rock, against which the powers of hell cannot prevail: that is to say, upon St. Peter, the chief of the Apostles, and upon the Roman Pontiffs his successors, the Supreme Vicars of JESUS Christ on earth.

Knowing, by revelation, that this Holy See was so chosen by the Divine Founder that it can never fail, we may say that by this election it has become the essential part of the Church of JESUS Christ, and that all other parts can only be regarded as accidental; for no infallible promise has been given that these parts, taken singly, may not for a time perish. Christians ought therefore to cherish in their hearts an unbounded affection, attachment, and reverence, for the Holy See of the Roman Pontiff. They ought, beyond all measure, to love and promote the true and holy glory, the honor and prosperity, of this essential part of the immaculate Spouse of JESUS Christ.

7. That part of the holy Church which has already reached its destination should be regarded by faithful Christians with a constant attraction and love, as

having attained its full perfection and splendour. They ought to excite in their hearts a desire, ever increasing, that all members of the Church, or those certainly that from eternity have been so predestined and chosen, may arrive at this final perfection; and that thus the whole kingdom of JESUS Christ may come, and be all assembled around Him, to complete His glory and His triumph throughout all ages. This is the divine will; in this has God placed His delight from all eternity: the same, therefore, should be the one final object of the Christian's desire, as it is the final object of the will of God.

8. But this cannot come to pass until all earthly things perish, until Christians shall die and their bodies be turned into dust, until the whole world shall be at last destroyed and judged. They will therefore desire this also, because they know that it is the means that God has appointed for obtaining the fullness of His glory and the great triumph of JESUS. And, as they ought always to bear in mind the glory of heaven, so also, in all their actions, they should remember that all things else decay, that they pass away quickly, and that death is the means of reaching their last rest in heaven.

9. Christians therefore will so live, as if on any day they might have to leave all things, as if at any moment they might die; not providing for the distant future, but keeping in their hearts those words of our Divine Master: *"See that you are dressed for action and have your lamps lit. Be like men waiting for their master to return from the wedding feast, ready to*

open the door as soon as he comes and knocks. Happy those servants whom the master finds awake when he comes. I tell you solemnly, he will put on an apron, sit them down at table and wait on them. It may be in the second watch he comes, or in the third, but happy those servants if he finds them ready. You may be quite sure of this, that if the householder had known at what hour the burglar would come, he would not have let anyone break through the wall of his house. You too must stand ready, because the Son of Man is coming at an hour you do not expect" (St. Luke 12, 35-40).

"We ought to love the Church beyond measure, prepared to shed our blood for Her"
(Relic of Blessed Antonio Rosmini – Beatification, Novara 2007)

THIRD MAXIM

"To remain perfectly at peace as to all that is ordained by God in regard to the Church of JESUS Christ, working for the Church in obedience to the divine Will."

THIRD MAXIM

"To remain perfectly at peace as to all that is ordained by God in regard to the Church of JESUS Christ, working for the Church in obedience to the divine Will."

1. JESUS Christ has power over all things in heaven and on earth, and has merited to be absolute Lord of all people; and He alone, with unspeakable wisdom, power and goodness, rules all events according to His Divine pleasure, and for the greater good of the elect who form His beloved Spouse the Church.

2. Christians therefore should feel perfectly at peace and full of joy, resting entirely upon their Lord, however contrary even to the good of the Church events may seem. But they must not cease from praying earnestly that the will of God may be done on earth as it is in heaven, that is, that people may fulfill the holy law of charity on earth as the saints fulfill it in heaven.

3. Christians should banish from their hearts all uneasiness, and every kind of anxiety and apprehension, even that which seems at times to have no other object than the good of the Church of JESUS Christ. Moreover, they must not rashly imagine that they can remedy the evils, which assail the Church, before they see clearly that such is the will of the Lord.

They must bear in mind that JESUS Christ alone is the Ruler of His Church, and that most displeasing to Him, and most unworthy of His disciples, is the rashness of those who, not called and moved by Him, but, led blindly by a secret pride, presume of their own accord to do any good in the Church, however little it may be, as if the Divine Redeemer stood in need of their poor help, or of that of any person whatever.

No one is necessary to the Divine Redeemer for the triumph of His Church, which is the salvation of mankind from the slavery of sin, in which all people without exception are immersed. It is only in His mercy, freely bestowed, that He chooses from among the redeemed those whom He pleases to raise to such an honour, in order to accomplish the greatest works, using often what is weakest and most contemptible in the eyes of the world.

4. In conclusion, let us sum up all that has been said as to the *end* that Christians ought to put before themselves, and ever to bear in mind in all their actions. We have seen that this end ought to be:

I - *Justice*, or holiness, in which consists the Divine glory;

II - The *Church* of JESUS Christ, as the means established by God to obtain that glory;

III - The *call* of JESUS Christ, as the One Who governs the Church in His wisdom as He pleases, so that she may give the greatest glory to God.

NOTE

Having thus purified their intentions, and set before them the *end* stated above, as that to which they are to direct all the actions of their life, the followers of

JESUS Christ must likewise know and fix the *means* of attaining the desired end. These they will find in regulating their conduct by the three maxims presented in the following instructions.

"JESUS Christ alone is the Ruler of His Church"
(Beatification of Blessed Rosmini, Novara 2007)

FOURTH MAXIM

*"To abandon ourselves
entirely to
Divine Providence"*

FOURTH MAXIM

"To abandon ourselves entirely to Divine Providence"

1- There is perhaps no other Maxim which helps more than this to obtain the peace of heart and evenness of mind proper to the Christian life.

2- There is perhaps no Maxim which, if it is practiced with the simplicity and generosity of heart that it requires, renders the follower of JESUS Christ more dear to the Heavenly Father. For it implies perfect confidence in Him, and in Him alone, complete detachment from all that appears delightful, powerful, and illustrious on earth, and a tender love, reserved for God alone.

It implies a most lively faith, which believes as certain that all things in the world, both great and small, rest alike in the hand of our Heavenly Father, and that nothing is done by them unless as disposed by Him for the accomplishment of His adorable designs. It implies also a belief in the infinite goodness, mercy, bounty, and generosity, of our Heavenly Father, Who disposes all things for the good of those who trust in Him; and Whose gifts, and favors, and care, and graces, are bestowed in proportion to the confidence of His well-beloved children.

3- There is no other Maxim that our Divine Master has recommended more by His words and example. Listen to the discourse which He made to His disciples, to console them in the persecutions to which they were to be subjected by the world:

"To you my friends I say: do not be afraid of those who kill the body and after that can do no more. I tell you whom to fear: fear him who, after he has killed, has the power to cast into hell. Yes, I tell you, fear him. Can you not buy five sparrows for two pennies? And yet not one is forgotten in God's sight. Why, every hair on your head has been counted. There is no need to be afraid: you are worth more than hundreds of sparrows..."

"That is why I am telling you not to worry about your life and what you are to eat, nor about your body and how you are to clothe it. For life means more than food, and the body more than clothing. Think of the ravens. They do not sow or reap; they have no storehouses and no barns; yet God feeds them. And how much more are you worth than the birds! Can any of you, for all his worrying, add a single cubit to his span of life? If the smallest things, therefore, are outside your control, why worry about the rest?

"Think of the flowers; they never have to spin or weave; yet, I assure you, not even Solomon in all his regalia was robed like one of these. Now if that is how God clothes the grass in the field which is there today and thrown into the furnace tomorrow, how much more will He look after you, you men of little faith! But you, you must not set your hearts on things to eat and things to drink; nor must you worry. It is the pagans of this world who set their hearts on all

these things. Your Father well knows you need them. No; set your hearts on his kingdom, and these other things will be given you as well.

There is no need to be afraid, little flock, for it has pleased your Father to give you the kingdom. Sell your possessions and give alms. Get yourselves purses that do not wear out, treasure that will not fail you, in heaven where no thief can reach it and no moth destroy it. For where your treasure is, there will your heart be also" (St. Luke 12, 4-7; 22-34).

How complete is this instruction of our Divine Master as to the way in which His faithful disciples should abandon themselves into the compassionate arms of Divine Providence!

From this instruction the disciples will learn, in the *first* place, that the foundation of their full and unbounded confidence is JESUS Himself: for He says, at the very beginning, that those to whom He addresses these words are His friends. And by friends He does not mean those only that are perfect, but all Christians, and, amongst Christians, even sinners. He calls those His friends whom He has treated as such, by revealing to them the Gospel.

For this reason everyone ought to be greatly comforted by the thought, that He did not refuse the name of friend even to Judas when he came to betray Him. Whoever, therefore, believes in JESUS, has in this object of belief a foundation for unlimited trust in the Heavenly Father, a trust which must not be shaken even by our sins.

Secondly, Christians will learn that, as it is reasonable to leave ourselves completely in the hands of the Divine goodness, so it is foolish to trust in ourselves. Human beings are extremely weak, and cannot change in the least the course which God has marked out for all things in the universe. Their prosperity and their existence are all in God's hands; and from those hands they cannot steal them away, whatever they may try to do, or wherever they may try to go, even were they able to ascend into the heavens above or to descend into the depths below.

Thirdly, they will learn that, having such reasons for an unlimited trust in their Heavenly Father, they should not fear even to give up all human things, to sell their possessions and give the proceeds to the poor, to profess, in fact, true poverty, if they do so for the purpose of attending only to divine things, of giving themselves totally to God, of seeking the kingdom of God and His justice, of freeing their hearts from all earthly affections, in a word, for the purpose of following Christ clinging to the blessed nakedness of His Cross, dying upon it to all earthly things, and living only for heavenly things; for where their treasure is, there will their hearts be also.

Fourthly, they will learn that, although they are forbidden to be unduly concerned about human things and are advised to give them up, yet they are not forbidden to ask their Heavenly Father for what is necessary, as long as they ask for it after first asking for His kingdom and His justice, and as a means to this end; so that the daily bread we ask for may in a right sense be called *super- substantial,* that is a means for obtaining also spiritual blessings.

9- Our divine Master says in another place, *"Ask, and it will be given to you; search, and you will find; knock, and the door will be opened to you. For the one who asks always receives; the one who searches always find; the one who knocks will always have the door opened to him. Is there a man among you who would hand his son a stone when he asked for bread? Or would hand him a snake when he asked for a fish? If you, then, who are evil, know how to give your children what is good, how much more will your Father in heaven give good things to those who ask Him!"* (St. Matt. 7, 7-11).

10- These words teach Christians to ask their Heavenly Father for all things with great simplicity and confidence, and to manifest to Him all the wishes of their hearts, provided that they do it with the sole desire that what is most pleasing to God may always come to pass. In this way they will always obtain great fruit from their prayers, because God, in graciously hearing them, will correct their ignorance and dullness of mind, should they ask for what is useless or harmful, granting instead what is truly beneficial to them, and even more than they have asked; for God is a Father, who knows how to give good things to His children, and never gives them what is harmful.

11- *Fifthly,* Christians will learn that they are not forbidden to do whatever is needed for satisfying the wants of life; what they are forbidden is to worry and to be anxious, becoming restless by longing for what they do not have, and thus losing the peace of heart and the serenity proper to those who have placed their trust in God.

Christians may see the divine will in the present conditions, and may enjoy in simplicity and with thanksgiving the good things they have. But anxious care about the future is opposed to a complete trust in Divine Providence, because, as to the future, the will of God is not yet manifest, and they ought to love nothing but the Divine will. This they can do with a moderate and innocent enjoyment of present good things, as given to them by God; but they must not be troubled about those of the future, for the Lord has not yet disposed concerning them. Thus, loving the Divine will, they will rejoice as much in the privation of these things, if it be so ordained, as in acquiring them.

12- For this reason Jesus also says: *"Set your hearts on his kingdom first, and on his righteousness, and all these other things will be given you as well. So do not worry about tomorrow; tomorrow will take care of itself. Each day has enough trouble of its own"* (St. Matt. 6, 33-34). That is, we must not increase the stains which our conscience acquires by worrying about the present, by being anxious also about tomorrow.

13- The sure way therefore by which Christians may know if they are lacking in that complete trust they are commanded to have in the provident care of their Heavenly Father, is to examine whether they feel any anxiety about good and evil in this world: whether they are always perfectly at peace and calm, and prepared for whatever it may happen; or whether they are subject to disquiet, whether they deal with human affairs with troubling worry about their result, and whether, as people of little faith, they have excessive hopes and fears, that is, they are always in a state of uncertainty.

14- *Sixthly,* since the perfection of the Christian life consists in a firm resolve to seek only, in everything we do, what is most pleasing to God and most in conformity with His will, and since this perfect life is nothing but a profession to give God in all our actions the greatest possible service, it follows, that, both the natural activities people do for the preservation of life, and even the enjoyment of God's gifts with a thankful heart, ought not to be done by them for the sake of their present benefit or pleasure, but only from a conviction that, given the circumstances in which they are placed, this is what is most dear to God, and what is therefore most perfect.

15- In a word, perfect Christians do not make changes for the sole purpose of an immediate pleasure, no matter how innocent it may be, but solely for the sake of duty, by means of which becoming dearer to God.

16- This Maxim is the source of the solidity of perfect Christians. They do not love change, they are happy and joyful in whatever condition they find themselves, however lowly and abject it may be, and destitute of all that other people care for. They do not consider any change unless they know it to be the will of God.

It is the characteristic of worldly people never to be satisfied with their state in life; they are always at war for the highest positions. Christian perfection, on the other hand, requires that Christians should be satisfied with any post whatever, and that they should have no other thought but to fulfill the duties belonging to their state. All things in this world are for them alike, so long as they can be dear to their God, Whom they find in every situation.

17- This constancy, this steadiness of Christians in the condition they find themselves, produces persons who are thoroughly acquainted with their state, who love it, and who know how to carry out all their duties. This is most fitting in view of the fleeting nature of human things, and for this reason St. Paul recommended it strongly to the Corinthians in these words:

"*Each one of you, my brothers, should stay as he was before God at the time of his call. About remaining celibate, I have no directions from the Lord but give my own opinion as one who, by the Lord's mercy, has stayed faithful. Well then, I believe that in the present time of stress this is right: that it is good for a man to stay as he is. If you are tied to a wife, do not look for freedom; if you are free of a wife, then do not look for one. But if you marry, it is no sin, and it is not a sin for a young girl to get married. They will have their troubles, though, in their married life, and I should like to spare you that. Brothers, this is what I mean;*

our time is growing short. Those who have wives should live as though they have none, and those who mourn should live as though they had nothing to mourn for; those who are enjoying life should live as though there were nothing to laugh about; those whose life is buying things should live as though they had nothing of their own; and those who have to deal with the world should not become engrossed in it. I say this because the world as we know it is passing away. I would like to see you free from all worry" (1 Cor. 7, 24-32).

18- *Seventhly,* and lastly, Christians who follow these rules of conduct will be equally willing and happy to change whenever the Divine will is known to them, or the will of their superiors who hold the place of God towards them; and their souls will always be rooted and maintained in that golden state of *indifference* so highly commended by St. Ignatius who made it the foundation of his Spiritual Exercises, and the basis of the whole spiritual life.

19- This indifference springs from the resolution not only to serve God, which is the end for which all human beings have been created; but, moreover, to serve Him in the way He wishes to be served by each of us, this being the primary means of achieving that great end.

20- Christians, in fact, who desire to serve God, not in the way chosen by themselves, but in the manner laid down and willed by God, will achieve a state of indifference (as far as their free will, though not their natural inclination, is concerned) regarding the four conditions distinguished so clearly by St. Ignatius. They are:

I- Indifference to health or to sickness;
II – Indifference to riches and comforts or to poverty of life;
III- Indifference to praise or to contempt from the world;
IV- Indifference to a long life or to a short life, shortened perhaps by toil and suffering.

21- The frequent examination of conscience under-taken by the disciples of JESUS Christ to discover whether they are truly indifferent to poverty or riches, to honour or contempt, to health or sickness, to a long or a short life, will enable them to see what progress they have made on their way to evangelical perfection.

22- This indifference, which should be the constant aim of faithful Christians, may also be reduced to the three following heads:

I – Indifference to any *work* assigned to them;
II – Indifference to any *place* in which to live;
III – Indifference to any *state* of health they may have.

"Set your hearts on His Kingdom"
(Pilgrims to S. Monte Calvario, Domodossola)

FIFTH MAXIM

"To acknowledge profoundly our own nothingness"

FIFTH MAXIM

"To acknowledge profoundly our own nothingness"

1- The disciples of JESUS Christ should always live in a state of interior solitude, in which, after the disappearance, so to speak, of all other things, they may find only God and their own soul.

2- They should have God always present, that they may adore His greatness; and they must be always aware of themselves, that they may know more thoroughly their own weakness and nothingness.

3- Christians should have the reasons of their own nothingness deeply impressed upon their minds: *firstly,* those that prove the nothingness of all created things; *secondly,* those that humble human beings in particular; and *thirdly,* those that humble each of them personally.

4- As each of them is an atom in comparison with the universe, so each of them is nothing in comparison with God, from Whom alone comes whatever good they have. The sin in which they were conceived, the inclination that they have to evil, and the sins they have committed, ought to convince them of two great truths:

I- By themselves they are incapable of doing any good;

II- Not only they are capable of every evil, but they are so frail that they may sin at any moment unless the Divine mercy comes to their aid, so that they ought always *"to work out their salvation with fear and trembling"*, as the Apostle says (Phil. 2, 12).

5- The first of these two great truths should dissuade them from undertaking anything, either in regard to a change in their state of life, of which we have already spoken, or for any other purpose, unless they know it to be the will of God. It is impossible for people to undertake anything of their own accord, if they sincerely believe to be incapable of any good.

6- Thus, there ought to be in Christians two dispositions that seem opposed to each other, but are yet in perfect agreement: that is to say, a most ardent zeal for the glory of God and for the good of their neighbour, and a conviction that, of themselves, they are incapable of doing any good, or of applying any remedy to the evils of the world.

7- They ought therefore to imitate the humility of Moses, who found it so hard to believe that he had been chosen to deliver the people of God, that he besought God, with affectionate simplicity and confidence, to relieve him of so great a charge because he was slow of tongue, and to send instead Him who was to be sent, namely the promised Messiah. Yet Moses was full of zeal for the salvation of his people.

Christians ought, moreover, to meditate on, and always to imitate, the most profound humility of the Blessed Virgin Mary, whom the Holy Scriptures describe as in a state of constant calm, and peace, and quietness. By her own choice, her life was humble, secluded, and silent: and she was drawn from it only by the voice of God, or by feelings of charity towards her cousin Elizabeth.

According to human judgment, who would believe that so little had been narrated in the Holy Scriptures of the most perfect of all human creatures? No great work was undertaken by her; yet her life, which the world in its blindness would regard as one of continued inaction, was declared by God to be the most sublime, the most virtuous, the most magnanimous of all lives; and for this reason the humble and unknown Virgin was raised by the Almighty to the highest dignity of all, and to a throne of glory more exalted than any that was ever given to human beings or even to the angels.

8- The *second* truth ought to produce in Christians a reasonable fear of the dangers with which the Holy Scriptures declare the world to be filled. John the Evangelist goes so far as to assure us that everything in the world is a danger.

9- Therefore Christians who wish to be perfect will lead a life of seclusion, of silence, and of constant occupation.

10- Their seclusion will involve a resolve not to leave their home without necessity; that is to say, unless either the duties of their state or a well founded charity towards their neighbour shall lead them to do so.

11- They will lead a life of silence, endeavouring not to utter idle words; that is, words which are not intended for their own spiritual benefit or that of others, or which are not required by the duties or needs of their own life.

12- Lastly, they will lead a life of constant occupation, so as never to lose the least moment of time. They will often reflect that time is most precious, that the moments which they allow to pass away without gaining from them some spiritual profit are beyond recall, that of those moments they will have to give an exact account to God, as of a talent that had been entrusted to them with which to trade.

They will reflect that continual occupation is in a special manner required of those who profess to lead a perfect life, because by such profession they resolve to attend immediately, and solely, and as much as possible, to the service of God, dedicating to it their whole time and strength.

"By ourselves we are incapable of doing any good but with Christ we can do all things"
(S. Monte Calvario, Blessed Rosmini's Room)

Sixth Maxim

"To regulate all the occupations of our life with a spirit of intelligence"

SIXTH MAXIM

"To regulate all the occupations of our life with a spirit of intelligence"

1- Christians should never walk in darkness, but always in the light.

2- For this reason they should pray continually to the Holy Spirit for the gift of *understanding,* by which they may attain a deeper grasp of the sublime truths of faith; the gift of *wisdom,* by which they may judge correctly of Divine things; the gift of *knowledge,* by which they may judge correctly of human things; and lastly the gift of *counsel,* by which they may direct themselves, by applying the truths they have learnt to the particular actions of their lives.

3- Christians should be distinguished by the gravity, thoughtfulness, and maturity they bring to bear on all things. They must avoid the haste and precipitation so typical of worldly people; for they are contrary to the gifts already mentioned, and come from a human will filled with that anxiety which destroys the peace so much recommended by our Divine Master.

4- The spirit of intelligence will lead Christians always to think first of their own purification, far more than of the purification of their neighbour.

5A- As to their own purification and perfection, the will of God will easily be made known to them; and first of all, they will find it in the circumstances in which they find themselves. Following this most sure principle, they will understand that,

I - The first thing the will of God lays down for them, is to fulfill with faithfulness, accuracy and promptness, all the duties of their state; to do whatever the relations to which they are bound to other people require of them, using that degree of love and respect that arises naturally from such relations; in short, to act towards them with so much charity that they will be well pleased with them.

They will converse with those with whom they have to deal (for their love of seclusion will make them reluctant to converse with those towards whom they have no obligation) with great gentleness, holy friendship, and real spiritual edification.

6- The same principle of fulfilling the duties of their state, and of spending well all their time, will make Christians fond of hard work, especially in their profession or occupation, in which they will be very diligent. If they make progress in their fields, they will look upon this as a source of merits in the sight of God, Whose will it is that they should do well all that is required by the state in which God has placed them.

7- If they are committed to the academic life, they will apply themselves to their studies not for the love of study in itself, but for the love of God, Whom alone they serve. If they are employed in a manual or technical job, they will work hard, for the same end. In this way, Christians will not regard one occupation as more noble or more lowly than another, because in every work they are serving the same God.

They will perform their tasks, as workmen in the great workshop of the same master; and at the end of the day they will receive their wages, not according to the type of work they had been doing, but according to the fidelity, diligence, and care with which they had done it, and the love they had shown to their Master.

8- II - Next to the duties of their state (including, of course, all their religious obligations) the disciples of JESUS Christ will give the rest of their time:

1- to spiritual reading, both for their own thorough instruction in the doctrines of faith, and for personal meditation on the greatness, the infinite goodness, the omnipotence, and the wisdom of God;

2- to spontaneous prayer, which they will practice for as long as possible, even during the various tasks of their ordinary occupation. Prayer should become familiar and most dear to them, more precious than everything else; and the time that they spend in prayer they should look upon as a time of delight and of grace; for human beings, worthless as they are, are admitted by prayer to an audience with the Divine Majesty, and allowed to converse intimately with God.

9- III - Christians may spend a part of their time in attending to their bodily needs, first among which are eating and sleeping. Their meals should be simple and ordinary, and their sleep should follow the rules of moderation.

10- Christians will also allow themselves a moderate amount of rest when tired, after the example of JESUS Christ who did all that was necessary to preserve life, and also of taking rest, as when He slept in the boat, and sat by the well in Samaria.

11- IV - The circumstances of their state and the relationships which bind them to others may be such as to put no obstacle to the practice of the evangelical counsels, that is, to the actual profession of poverty, chastity, and obedience. In this case, Christians who earnestly desire to resemble their Divine Model as closely as possible, and to neglect nothing that their Divine Master has recommended as belonging to a life of perfection, will embrace these counsels with courage and eagerness. If they are free to do so, they will practice all three of them; if not, they will take up one or two of them as circumstances permit.

12- B –Although Christians, of their own accord, do not seek to do anything great, for they really believe to be incapable of anything good; and although they are wholly devoted to the duties of their state, and although they choose a secluded, and, as far as possible, a solitary, silent, and hidden life, nonetheless they are not in the least unconcerned about the good and bad things endured by their neighbour. They pray for them and ardently long for their good; and they are always ready to spend and to sacrifice their whole life for their spiritual salvation, when they have good reason to believe that what they do for them is not done out of their own reckless initiative, but only because it is required of them by God.

13- Thus, the spirit of intelligence should guide Christians to know the will of God concerning the work they should do for the benefit of their brethren.

14- The same spirit of intelligence teaches them that, even in regard to the duties of charity towards their brethren, the will of God is primarily and ordinarily made known by means of external circumstances.

15- These are the circumstances by which they may know with confidence which particular act of charity God is calling them to exercise towards their neighbour:

I- When the needs of their neighbour are open before their own eyes, for St. John says clearly: *"If a man who was rich enough in this world's goods saw that one of his brothers was in need, but closed his heart to him, how could the love of God be living in him?"* (1 John 3, 17)

II- When their neighbour ask them for some charitable service, for the same Divine Master who said in one place, *"You must be perfect, as your Heavenly Father is perfect"* (St. Matt. 5, 48), in another place told us that our Heavenly Father will give us anything we ask in His name. Christians therefore who want to be perfect as their Heavenly Father is perfect, must give all they can, when their neighbour ask it of them.

16- To perform well the work of charity they have been asked to do, they must do it with courage and cheerfulness, if indeed it is their desire to respond fully to their vocation of a life of perfect charity. They will engage in the work even at the cost of serious personal discomfort and sacrifice, with that fervent love that leads a person to forget one's interests to think always of the interests of others.

They will do it with that perfect love our Divine Master showed towards all human beings, a love which was not constrained by human weakness, but which led Him, instead, to the shedding of His Blood on the Cross.

17- In this way, it can happen that humble and fervent Christians who would never think of choosing for themselves but a hidden life, withdrawn from the dangers of the world - a life of continuous contemplation, marked by assiduous prayer and study, or the exercise of a manual or technical profession, by attention to the necessities of life, and by a few moments of rest – such Christians are drawn by the force of charity from their seclusion, which they love not through sloth but through sincere humility, and are led into an active life, immersed, if such be the will of God, into a boundless sea of cares and troubles, of dealings and activities, important or unimportant, lofty or lowly, all for the good of their neighbour, and in the order decided for them by the will of God.

18- By means of the spirit of intelligence, Christians who are full of charity rise in these circumstances above themselves, and undertake very great, and most difficult and perilous tasks, anything, in fact, provided that God gives them the inner conviction that they are capable of achieving such things, and their superiors do not forbid them, and when they are asked either expressly or tacitly for these services by their neighbour, in whom they always see their Divine Lord.

19- Christians who love perfection undertake these works of charity without a voluntary preference for one rather than another.

20- They observe therefore the following three rules:

I - They undertake the first works of charity that their neighbour asks of them and never refuse them, whether they are great or small, pleasant or disagreeable, of a kind that could be done by any person or by themselves alone, for the sake of uncertain works of charity in the future.

II – If they are asked simultaneously to take on several works of charity that they cannot perform at the same time, they make their choice according to the *order of charity*, taking care however to undertake only those which are proportioned to their strength.

III – They do not become weary of any work of charity, or come to dislike it, but bring it to completion if they can. If the works they have undertaken require continuous occupation, they persevere in them, without passing to anything else, fulfilling their vocation by staying with them.

21- The will of God, besides being manifested in the more ordinary way, by external circumstances, may also be made known by extraordinary internal inspirations, provided, however, the external circumstances do not clearly indicate the contrary.

22- Christians therefore may go against the knowledge of their own nothingness, and may undertake works different from those that are suggested to them by their state of life, by means of inner promptings by the Holy Spirit, through which the divine will is clearly made known to them.

23- However, such inspirations ought to be well tested, and the secrets of our hearts examined, so that we may not be misled by self-love or deceived by the devil who sometimes transforms himself into an angel of light. Lastly, it is of great help to have these inspirations confirmed by our spiritual superiors.

24- The general and infallible rule for ascertaining the Divine will, whether manifested by external circumstance or by internal inspirations, is the peace and inner satisfaction which Christians experience deep down in their conscience.

With inner recollection, they must examine attentively whether they feel any restlessness. By this means, if they are careful, they will find an indication of their real state. Self-love, or any purely human motive, always causes in persons some little disquiet of conscience. When this is perceived, they will be able, if they wish, soon to find out its cause; and to detect in themselves what does not proceed from the pure spirit of God, which is a spirit of perfect calm, but from their own spirit, from a subtle pride, from a sensitiveness not wholly subdued, in a word, from a deception of the devil.

25- If Christians, following the teaching of their Divine Master, would put in practice all that has been set forth in this book, they would form a peaceful and happy society, not only in the life to come, but even in the present life.

"Christians should never walk in darkness, but always in the light"